Maker's Mark®

The Toll House

My Autobiography

Bill Samuels, Jr.

SABER PUBLISHING

Maker's Mark—My Autobiography © 2000 by Jim Lindsey and Saber Publishing
All Rights Reserved.

ISBN 0-9705861-0-8

Printed in Korea

Saber Publishing
c/o Regency Books/Butler Books
10344 Bluegrass Parkway
Louisville, KY 40299

Maker's Mark®, SIV®, the SIV Device, and the Dripping Wax Device are all registered trademarks of Maker's Mark Distillery, Inc.

Special thanks to Barbara Dutschke for her creative help, and to Barb Renfroe for all her research and hard work.

Finally, to Jim Lindsey, my advertising and marketing guru for 25 years, for his help in gathering the material, collaborating with me on the writing, and managing the entire book project.

This book is dedicated to Marty Jewett
(b. 1940, d. 1999), the genius behind the
friendly look and graphic personality of
Maker's Mark.

A great art director and a good friend—
we will miss him.

Introduction

Bourbon has its origins in the arrival of a unique group of immigrants to the young American colonies. The first settlers were from England and were accustomed to drinking beer and gin. Another group from Scotland and Ireland drank whisky, and they brought with them the skills to make it. They settled in Pennsylvania, Maryland and Virginia, and began distilling whisky from whatever grain was available, including Indian corn or maize.

It was a useful way to use surplus grain, and provided the distiller with a commodity he could trade. It was also easier to ship and to store in liquid form. It was one of America's first "value-added" products.

In 1791, George Washington imposed the first tax on whisky in order to raise desperately needed revenue for his administration. Ironically, Washington himself was a noted distiller in his home state of Virginia.

True to form, the Scots and Irish distillers, among the young country's most loyal citizens, revolted. Their angry protests became known as the Whisky Rebellion and Washington was forced to send in the militia to quell the conflict and collect the tax.

Many distillers refused to pay the tax and instead pushed westward into the area that was to become the state of Kentucky. They carved out new farms from the wilderness, far from the reach of Washington's tax collectors. They settled along the limestone belt that starts in Pennsylvania and extends into the flatlands of central Kentucky, knowing that this mineral watershed assured them the pure, iron-free water they needed to distill whisky. My great-great-great-great grandfather, Robert Samuels, was one of them.

His grandfather, John, was of Scots-Irish descent who made only enough whisky each year to keep himself and a few close friends satisfied.

The first whiskies were made from whatever grains were at hand. However, as the markets became more sophisticated, distinctions began to be made about the quality of the available whiskies.

In 1840, Robert Samuels' grandson, T.W. Samuels, erected the family's first commercial distillery near Samuels Depot, Kentucky, on the family farm. Just as his ancestors had, T.W. Samuels passed the family's secret whisky-making formula along to my great-grandfather, who passed it along to my grandfather.

But my father didn't like our family whisky very much. He thought it was "pedestrian whisky." He was determined to create his own style of bourbon whisky—one that was soft, smooth, clean and pleasant to the taste buds.

He started over in 1953 by purchasing, then rebuilding, a small old distillery fed by clear, clean, limestone springs in picturesque Happy Hollow, near Loretto, Kentucky. There he set about turning his dream into reality.

He began by changing the sacred family formula. In the process, he may have reinvented bourbon whisky. His new formula was comprised of corn grown in soil with a composition identical to that of the distillery, coupled with locally grown gentle winter wheat—not the traditional distiller's rye.

And, although dissatisfied with the old family recipe and the product that resulted from it, Dad remained committed to the family values passed down through the years. The whisky would be handcrafted in small quantities by men and women, not by machines or computers.

It would be a whisky made in such small batches that he could be choosy about everything he used and everything he did to craft his bourbon before it went into the barrel.

The result would be Maker's Mark.

This is the story of how it all came about. I was there, and now I would like to share it with you.

Bill Samuels, Jr.

Bill Samuels, Jr.
President
Maker's Mark Distillery, Inc.

The Adventure Begins.

My father was an introspective man and a true craftsman. After World War II, he became Vice President and General Manager of the T.W. Samuels distillery. Our family whisky.

All was well and good, I guess, except that the whisky wasn't very good. It really never had been very good. But, it didn't seem to matter.

American whisky, or "red whisky" as they used to call it in the 1800s, wasn't for the faint of heart. Cowboys coming off three months on the trail weren't looking for a wine spritzer.

The whisky had bite and bitterness and a sour aftertaste. Bourbon was always the unrefined uncle at the family party. Then came 1920 and American Prohibition. The distilleries shut down. Rum, Canadian whiskey and scotch flowed across American

borders by way of the bootleggers, rumrunners and whatever else you might want to call them.

In 1934, when Prohibition was over, the American distilleries jumped headlong back into the marketplace in too big a hurry with whisky that was under-aged and pretty terrible. The vast majority of bourbons were again to be categorized as rough, tough, and unpleasant on the palate.

Such was the family whisky, and dad was not pleased about it. The imported liquors were viewed as much more sophisticated and much more palatable. In 1943, he decided to get out and risk everything on the single idea that there was a way to craft a bourbon whisky that would be smooth as velvet, full-flavored and easy on the palate.

The saga of Maker's Mark begins with that dream—a vision of what many people have come to believe is the very best bourbon whisky in the world.

You be the judge.

No Turning Back Now.

Soon after deciding to buy the old Burks distillery and beginning to fashion his idea of a new kind of bourbon whisky, Dad performed a ceremony that rather shocked us all. He burned the only copy of our old family whisky formula.

He made quite a production of torching the 170-year-old recipe that had gained our family some renown in the whisky business. "Nothing that we need! To craft a truly new and soft-spoken bourbon," he declared, "we will have to start from scratch." Then, in front of my mother, my sisters, our three employees and me, he put a match to it.

Unfortunately, in the process he also set fire to our drapes which in turn nearly set fire to one of my sisters. Understandably, we never talked much about "the ceremony" in front of my father.

> "Maker's Mark goes against the grain to make its mark. Bill Samuels started from scratch and established a brand of superior quality with a fine image."
> David P. Garino
> *The Wall Street Journal*

The Birthplace of Maker's Mark.

My father began creating Maker's Mark by baking bread. Lots and lots of bread. He experimented with corn and wheat and all sorts of rye and barley combinations.

It takes about five or six years to bring a bourbon whisky to maturity— that is, to a state where it is rounding into maturity and you can taste it. Trial-and-error experimenting to determine just the right formula could take a lifetime.

So dad made bread from various grains to get a feel for the balance he was looking for in the new formula. He wanted none of the "hot, raspy, bitter" taste traditionally associated with bourbon whisky.

So instead of using rye which is the traditional "flavor" grain in bourbon distilling, my father substituted soft winter wheat. He explained it this way: "Imagine two loaves of bread, one made from whole wheat, the other from rye. Isn't the bread made from wheat lighter, milder and more gentle on the palate?"

Judging from what people tell me, I guess Dad found the taste he was looking for. Even if we did have to eat a lot of pretty weird bread along the way.

Mom Named All of the Children and the Family Whisky.

While my father can take full credit for crafting the soft, full-flavored, distinctive taste of Maker's Mark, it was Mom who actually named our whisky.

We were sitting around the living room trying to come up with a name for our new whisky, and my father felt strongly about abandoning the age-old practice of using the family name. You know, like Jim Beam, Jack Daniels, I.W. Harper, etc.

Well, Mom said that any craftsman worth his salt puts his name on his work. And so the debate continued through the evening.

She was a collector of fine English pewter and she knew that accomplished silversmiths and pewtersmiths put their

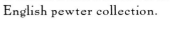
A maker's mark from Mom's English pewter collection.

personal mark only on their
very best work. She walked
over to the mantel, picked up
an old English pewter bottle,
turned it over, rubbed her
thumb across the stamped

Any time you're in the neighborhood, stop by and visit us at our
distillery, near Loretto, Kentucky.
Built in 1889 and beautifully restored, the home of Maker's Mark
is a designated Kentucky and
National Historic Landmark.

Fully Matured
750 ml. (25.4 fl.oz.)
alcohol 45% by volume
(Ninety Proof)

Maker's Ⓢ IV Mark®

KENTUCKY STRAIGHT BOURBON
WHISKY
OLD STYLE SOUR MASH

Distilled, aged and bottled by the
Maker's Mark Distillery, Inc.
on Star Hill Farm, Loretto, Ky.
45% Alc./Vol.

Maker's Mark is the world's
only bourbon made in small
quantities of less than 19
barrels per batch.
Which means we can afford to
be choosy about everything
we use and everything we do to
craft our bourbon.
You see, we keep a watchful eye
on every kernel of corn, every
grain of special winter wheat
and every drop of limestone
spring water we use.
It's a process that involves lots
of time. Lots of patience. And
most important, the human touch.
If all of this sounds a little too
obsessive, have a sip of Maker's
Mark. You may find its remarkable taste just might be worth
all the fuss.

symbol on the bottom and said,
"See this? It's the mark of the
craftsman. It's his maker's
mark." Dad said, "Okay."
And that's how my father came
to apply his seal of approval
instead of his name to our
family whisky.

Maker's Mark.

And we all went to bed.

The Maker's Mark.

After Mom came up with the name for our new family whisky, Dad had to come up with the maker's mark.

He started with the name of our old family farm in Bardstown, Kentucky—Star Hill Farm. Then he added an S to stand for the Samuels family name, and last he added IV to signify his place in the family line of distillers—fourth generation.

And so our name and trademark were born and remain unchanged today.

Here I am still wet behind the ears with Dad in front of a bronze plaque at the distillery. Dad is last on the plaque behind us, taking his place as the fourth generation Samuels' family distiller. He's really the sixth.

18

OOPS !

I was always deeply interested in our family history, even as a
boy. So, after I graduated from law school, I took it upon myself to do our family genealogy. What I found was a much
longer history of whisky-making than we had thought. My
great-great-grandfather was the first of our family distillers to
incorporate, but not the first to make and sell bourbon. He was
a third-generation distiller himself.

So my dad was the sixth, not the fourth, generation of distillers
and our trademark has been wrong all these years. Well, at
least it has been only a bit inaccurate. But that's all part of our
history now, and we don't intend to change it. Even when my
son Rob takes over one of these days.

I'm the seventh-generation distiller in the Samuels family
line and I'm glad to set the record straight.

I'm proud of our family history of distilling
American whisky. But I'm even more proud of
what we do at Maker's Mark today and what
our friends and customers think about
our whisky.

19

My Mother, the Package Designer.

My mother was the one who came up with the distinctive design of the Maker's Mark package. And now, more than 40 years later, she seems to be getting some well-deserved credit. In a recent competition, a panel of world-renowned graphic designers judged her liquor package design as one of the "Best 5" in the world.

Among other comments, a New York judge noted, "Every bottle is manually inverted in hot wax, which acts as a seal and becomes a clever design feature as the wax drips down the upright bottle. This tendril effect means each bottle is genuinely unique."

Of course, Mom would've never used words like that to describe her idea, but at least she is getting some long over-due recognition.

Besides fine pewter, Mom also collected 19th century bottles of cognac, many of which were sealed in colorful wax. Great idea, she thought. So she got out the family deep fryer, filled it with wax and dipped the first bottles right in our kitchen. Our production line has been the slowest in the industry ever since.

She also came up with the original design for the label. She liked things simple and chose black hand lettering on cream-colored paper.

She even helped design the bottle. Round or square would have been too mundane and too easy, I guess.

And she insisted that our new trademark seal had to be molded into the glass of each bottle of Maker's Mark.

Maker's Mark
Distillery

NATIONAL HISTORIC LANDMARK

First started as a gristmill in

If Utopia is defined as a place where everything is perfect, then we think it's here among the rolling fields of Marion County, Kentucky, where my father first began to craft Maker's Mark. Without the hustle and bustle of the city to distract him, he could mull over ideas until they were just right. That's how he came up with such a novel way of making a truly handmade bourbon.

With an atmosphere that nurtures such wonderful ideas, I can't imagine making Maker's Mark anywhere else.

Welcome to Utopia.

Painting of the Maker's Mark distillery by the well-known artist, David McCall Johnston. It was painted in 1989 and is now on display at the distillery.

23

The Home of Maker's Mark.

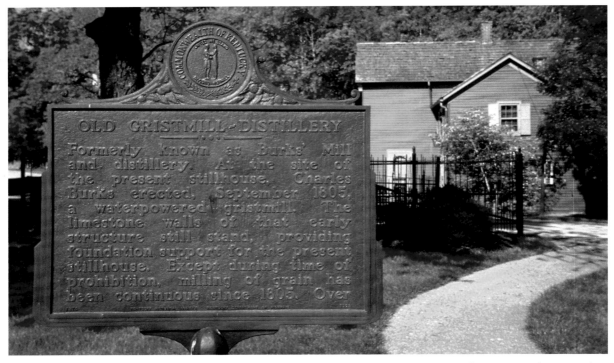

After years of loving restoration, what my father envisioned in 1953 can now be seen and enjoyed by all. You're always invited to come and see for yourself.

The world's only trapezoidal covered bridge spans Whisky Creek, which meanders through the distillery.

(Below) The Arboretum. Today the beautifully manicured grounds are home to over 275 species of trees and shrubs. Bring a picnic lunch and enjoy it in our idyllic setting.

(Left) The Still House, the heart of Maker's Mark. This is where you can see our bourbon being made by hand every step of the way.

(Below) The scenic little creek that once powered the original grist mill back in the early 1900s still runs through the middle of our little distillery, although it's not used to run the mill anymore.

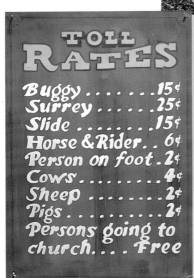

The Toll House. A reminder of the days when fees were levied for the use of our little country road nearly a century ago. Don't worry. Today you can drive into our distillery absolutely free.

(Right) The Barrel Warehouse is one of our many warehouses. After the barrels are filled, we store them here.

(Below) The Fire Department. We have our own antique fire engine and fire house. It's a popular spot for pictures and a handy backup for us in case of an emergency.

(Left and below) The Visitor's Center. This is where our distillery tours start and end. Inside you can also shop in our gift gallery and even try your hand at dipping your own souvenir bottle of Maker's Mark.

(Below) The Original Owner's House. This fully restored, beautiful Victorian home still stands on the hill overlooking the distillery.

The Quart House.

It is believed to be America's oldest remaining "retail package liquor store." Back in the late 1800s, neighbors would stop by with their quart jars, jugs, crocks, and pails to have them filled from the whisky casks kept here for that

purpose. I'm sure they were in no big hurry and probably stayed awhile to chat about the day's events and the price of grain.

The inside of the Quart House (left) has been authentically restored to reflect a period well before Prohibition. Be sure to see it when you visit the distillery.

An Operating National Historic Landmark Distillery.

In 1953, my father bought a 200-acre plot of land in Happy Hollow, Kentucky. No kidding. It's located near Loretto.

Located on the site was a small, quaint, run-down distillery which he immediately began to restore. Dad's goal was to create a bourbon that was a kinder and gentler alternative to the current batch of bourbons on the market, yet with a rich, robust, full-flavored taste.

This charming little Victorian distillery would be the "perfect home" for the

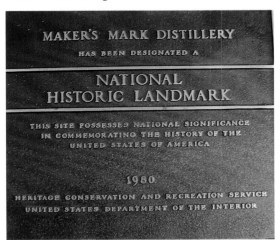

"perfect whisky" he was set on creating. In the late 1960s, Dad and I began the restoration in earnest with the intent to do it right—restoration, not decoration. We wanted a facility as distinctive as our bourbon.

Eleven years, much sweat, and two million dollars later, our efforts were recognized by then U.S. Secretary of Interior, Cecil Andress, who presented us with a plaque certifying Maker's Mark as a National Historic Landmark.

How My Great-Great-Grandfather Ended the Civil War.

It wasn't until 1840 that my great-great-grandfather T.W. Samuels erected the family's first real commercial distillery near Samuels Depot, Kentucky. It was on our family farm.

The whisky business was going pretty good and so was everything else until late April in 1865. General Robert E. Lee had surrendered to General Grant at Appomattox and the Civil War was supposedly over. But William Clark Quantrill's band of Confederate irregulars had other ideas.

T.W. Samuels, our third generation family distiller and High Sheriff of Nelson County, Kentucky.

The Quantrill guerrillas, including Jesse and Frank James, doggedly continued to attack Union sympathizers throughout central Kentucky. Eventually, however, Quantrill was shot and his irregulars were chased to the hamlet of Samuels, Kentucky.

(Left) A rare photograph of William Quantrill, the captain in the Confederate Army and leader of a notorious band of guerrillas known for their ruthless attack on the town of Lawrence, Kansas, and their raids on communities sympathetic to the Union cause all over Kansas, Missouri and Kentucky.

They took refuge at the home of my great-great-grandfather, who was not only a distiller but also the High Sheriff, as well as the cousin of Jesse and Frank's stepfather. After an all-night discussion in the kitchen, Frank was persuaded that it was best to trust his safety to a family member and best to lay low for awhile until the heat was off.

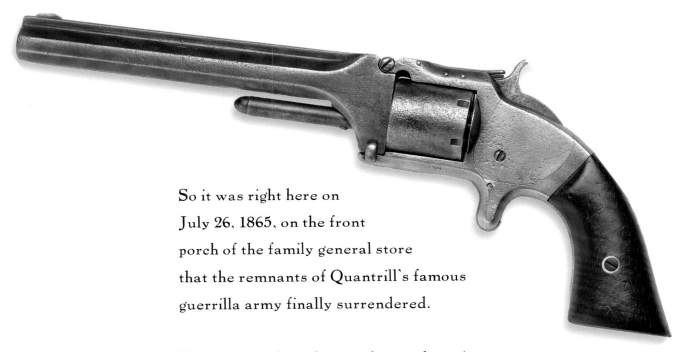

So it was right here on July 26, 1865, on the front porch of the family general store that the remnants of Quantrill's famous guerrilla army finally surrendered.

They received pardons and went down in history as the last Confederate soldiers to surrender in the War Between the States.

(Above) Smith and Wesson Model #2 six-shot .32 caliber cartridge revolver similar to the one carried by General Robert E. Lee, and the one alleged to have been carried by William Quantrill when he was shot in Kentucky.

You can't pick your relatives. And, I'm afraid we're related to Jesse and Frank James.

Jesse Woodson James, an American outlaw whose exploits are legendary. He joined Quantrill's Raiders at age 15 during the Civil War and earned a reputation for reckless daring.

Cousin Reuben Samuels married the widow James back when her sons, Frank and Jesse, were small boys. Later, as adults, both boys visited frequently with their cousins in Kentucky.

After they surrendered to my great-great-grandfather at Samuels Depot in 1865, Frank turned his Colt revolver over to my great-great-aunt, Ora Samuels.

Donnie and Bud Pence, two others in Quantrill's bunch, stayed on and married the High Sheriff's pretty lady cousins and, after a brief time in the James Gang, became law officers in Kentucky. Bud became the town marshal in Taylorsville and Donnie succeeded my great-great-grandfather as High Sheriff of Nelson County.

After mustering out of Quantrill's rebel band after the war, the James

The James Farm near Kearney, Missouri about 1884. From the left are Dr. Reuben Samuels, "Pinky," a farmhand, Zerelda Samuels, mother of Frank and Jesse, and Norma Samuels, their daughter-in-law.

Alexander Franklin James. This photo of Frank was taken in his later years, after Jesse's death.

.36 caliber bullets.

(Below) Frank's .36 caliber 1851 Navy Colt cap-and-ball revolver, surrendered to my great, great grandfather at Samuels Depot, Kentucky, in 1865.

brothers turned to crime. They robbed the Southern Deposit Bank in Russelville, Kentucky, and escaped with $17,000 even though the President of the bank had financed the education of the boys' father, Robert James, at Georgetown College.

Jesse even robbed one of his lady friends and her father on a stagecoach near Cave City, Kentucky. He was still wearing her father's pocket watch when he was killed years later.

Although the James boys came to visit often in the years that followed, they never stayed for long. But I spent many hours with my aunts who knew them well, and their stories still burn brightly in my memory. They are some of my best memories.

Frank's 1851 Navy Colt revolver is on display at the distillery. I used to play with it as a boy before we knew it was a piece of American history.

Kentucky Champagne.

We've come a long way since we dipped that first bottle of Maker's Mark in red wax heated up in Mom's deep fryer. And, Dad gained quite a reputation for turning traditional bourbon distilling upside down in the years between 1953, when he started his quest to craft a smooth, agreeable bourbon, and 1958, when our first bottle was dipped and sealed.

Today people tell me Maker's Mark has become a metaphor for good taste and a symbol of honest quality from Kentucky. I hope so. Dad would have been very proud to see the fruits of his labor grow to such proportions, even though he was a quiet and introspective man who would have preferred to leave it to others to tout the quality of his bourbon.

Which brings me to Robert Lawrence Balzer, former editor of Travel Holiday Magazine. While having dinner in a prominent Lexington, Kentucky restaurant, Mr. Balzer asked the waiter to bring him some Kentucky Champagne. He was served Maker's Mark in a brandy snifter. I love that story.

So, with all this success, I think we should take a closer look at what Dad did to come up with such a comfortable bourbon with such a pleasant taste.

Mom and Dad with the very first bottle of Maker's Mark, signed by all of the employees of the company in 1958.

A Handmade Whisky.

These days with all the bourbon distillers trying to find a way to make their products stand out, things can get pretty confusing. There's "Single Barrel" bourbon, "Small Batch" bourbon, "Single Warehouse" bourbon and a hoard of other descriptions.

Our Scotch/Irish heritage not only dictated the way we spell "whisky" (instead of the more generally used "whiskey"), it also dictated that Dad would make his bourbon in small, manageable batches of no more than 1,000 gallons

Dad and I sample a "batch" of Maker's Mark. Taste dictates everything we do as we craft our family whisky.

each—about 19 barrels. That's how small batch or handmade whisky is generally described in Scotland, and it's a far cry from the mass production techniques used in large distilleries.

Dad knew that making his whisky in small quantities meant that he could be careful about everything he did to craft his bourbon and choosy about every ingredient that he used along the way. Each little batch could be managed on its own as it went through the production process and the aging process.

He was sure that it was the only way to get the soft, full-flavored taste he was looking for. Today, Maker's Mark is still the only handmade bourbon in the world. It's slow and time-consuming, but I'm sure that it's the only way to make a truly great whisky.

"Small batches suggest a more carefully made, less industrial product that commands a higher price. Maker's Mark originated the breed and has been a leader in this category." Florence Fabricant, *The New York Times*

Checking the whisky as it ages.

Our Water is Pretty Exclusive.

Pure, iron-free limestone spring water has always been a critical element in the production of fine bourbon whisky. This special water is found primarily in a region running from north central Kentucky through, and including, south central Tennessee, thus explaining why most "bourbon style" whiskies have always come from this area.

At the time of the Civil War (1861-65), there were over 250 operating distilleries in this region. All got their whisky-making water from the nearby iron-free limestone springs. Today, there are just a few distillers left. And, while they are getting larger, the springs aren't. Other sources had to be found, even though none were as good as pure, iron-free limestone spring water.

Long ago, many of the other distilleries in our region began supplementing their spring water with water from other sources. We don't.

Dad believed that the water was the life's blood of good whisky. That's one of the main reasons he chose to make his whisky in Happy Hollow. It boasted a deep, clear spring-fed lake as part of the property. He decided to limit production of his whisky to the amount of water the springs could provide.

To this day, every drop of our bourbon is made only with the clean, limestone-filtered water from our spring-fed lake.

The Grain Holds a Secret.

Maker's Mark has a very distinctive grain formula. We use no rye in our formulation. Dad felt that rye had to be eliminated in order to soften his whisky. Through much experimentation, mostly by baking bread in our family kitchen, he concluded that winter wheat was the perfect choice to replace the rye.

The result was a gentler, softer and more pleasing bourbon whisky. A whisky with so little bite, and so little bitterness, you can actually hold it on your tongue at 90 proof.

Our grain ingredients are corn, winter wheat and barley malt. All of the

corn and wheat is selected from hand-picked area farms that have the same sort of limestone soil content as our spring water. We carefully check and hand-pick each truckload, and send back anything that doesn't meet our quality standards.

People often ask me if winter wheat makes such a difference, and why other distilleries don't copy us. Well, I suspect the answer is that it's not very easy. Wheat does not lend itself to mass production.

We simmer our grains for hours in a large cooking pot. We can manage each batch a little differently based on the characteristics of the grain in that particular batch. That's the only way we know to insure that the grain is not over-cooked.

Some other distilleries, because of their volume of production, fast forward this process in pressure cookers for speed and efficiency.

Well, wheat and pressure cookers just don't mix. It's a delicate grain that likes to get more than its share of attention. We try to accommodate it.

The Old Roller Mill.

Every distillery I know uses a modern hammer mill to break up their grains—except us, of course. We use an old antique roller mill to do the job.

The hammer mill is much more efficient because it completely pulverizes the grain into the consistency of face powder. These extra fine particles convert into more whisky than the old roller mill particles which are more coarse and are also slower to produce.

Grain made from our old roller mill.

The problem is that all of that pulverizing heats up the grain and often scorches it a little. And, as any good cook can tell you, scorching creates a bitter taste in the end product.

Our old roller mill is temperamental but we like the gentle way it grinds our grain into meal—slow, coarse and inefficient.

And, the whisky sure does taste good.

The Yeast.

Yeast is the catalyst in the whisky-making process. It's the ingredient that gets everything else cranked up and ready to go. Most distillers buy a stock product yeast and plug it into their formula, just as you would if you were making bread at home.

Well, not us. Our yeast strain is all our own and goes back almost 50 years to our first bottle of Maker's Mark. In fact, our yeast strain turns out to be three separate strains, growing and blending together.

We store it in a locked box in several specially constructed jugs weighing as much as 73 pounds each. Each holds several gallons of yeast cells, and we keep them dormant at 40 degrees fahrenheit. Why?

We believe that propagating our own yeast culture produces a unique effect during the process where grain sugars are converted to what we call ``Distiller's Beer.`` We think it's one of the details that contributes to the unique taste of Maker's Mark.

After the yeast has been added to the fermenting vat, we take special care to restart it in one of the six storage jugs and put it back to sleep until we need it again to start the next batch of Maker's Mark.

White Dog.

The cooked grains are mixed with the yeast in one of our open fermenting vats. The yeast goes to work on the fermentable sugars from the grain and produces a thing called "Distiller's Beer."

After three or four days in the fermenting vat, the mixture turns over. We call this "showing off," and it's a signal to start distilling the "beer."

Each vat is sized to produce about 19 bar-rels of unfinished whisky—a batch that will be identified by a lot number. Each lot will be followed and cared for throughout its time at the distillery based on its own unique characteristics.

The Still Tower.

(Below) An open fermenting vat with the yeast hard at work on the grains.

After leaving the vat, the fermented mash is moved to the still tower and mixed with steam in what is the tallest part of our little distillery.

This first distillation is at 120 proof—the lowest in the industry. This preserves the delicate taste and aroma of the wheat. It then goes to a doubler for a second distillation at a still low 130 proof.

The result is a crystal clear product we call ``White Dog''—Maker's Mark at one day old.

(Above) Checking ``White Dog'' as it comes through the tail box after distillation.

(Right) Crystal-clear ``White Dog.''

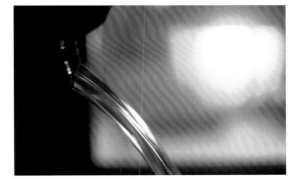

Even Our Barrels Get Special Treatment.

Once a batch of "white dog" has been distilled, it is carefully sampled, and its characteristics are recorded with the batch number. The new spirits are then diluted to 110 proof with a demineralized version of the same spring water that was used to make the mash.

Maker's Mark is put into the barrel at a lower proof than any other bourbon whisky made. Why? Well, it's not cost effective or very efficient but it does make for a better whisky. If your barrel proof is higher, you can get more finished whisky per barrel in the production process. We believe that if your barrel proof is lower, you get more flavor in your finished whisky.

The barrels we use are made from select American white oak. But, we do another thing different from the other distillers. We require our barrel maker to air-dry each wooden barrel stave outdoors for nine months, including one summer, before starting to make our barrels.

This adds considerably to the production cost, but we feel strongly that it also reduces the bitterness of the tannins in the wood and protects the soft-spoken character and flavor of our whisky.

48

The barrels are then assembled and charred on the inside. The charring concentrates the flavors and color in the oak into what we call "the red line." It lies just behind the charring which will act much like a charcoal filter as the whisky ages over the warm Kentucky summers that will follow.

We Encourage Stealing at Maker's Mark.

I'm proud to say that we employ a lot of thieves at our little distillery. Not the human kind, mind you. The copper tool kind.

A whisky thief is an old device that siphons bourbon from the barrel so you can take a taste. Just like people, barrels of bourbon don't mature at the same rate. Every batch is a little different and unique in its own right—so are the Kentucky summers.

Computers don't work here. The only accurate way to measure the aging process is to sample the bourbon and make decisions based on how each batch tastes along the way.

So, we use walnut bungs to plug our whisky barrels. Everyone else uses poplar bungs. Why? Because they're softer and seal tighter. They're not coming out until bottling time when they have

Real "whisky thief" in use in the warehouse.

to be drilled out. The calendar
determines when their whisky is ready.

Well, as they say, it's not how old you are but
how you've aged. That's why we believe
you have to taste the whisky inside
those barrels rather than rely on the
calendar. The hard walnut bungs we
use allow us to periodically open the
barrels and sample the whisky to
determine where each batch should
be moved in the warehouse for the
next year or two of aging, and to
determine when it has reached its peak
of maturity.

Our removable walnut bung.

Only then do we select it for bottling.

Maker's Mark is
crystal clear when it
goes into the barrel
and a beautiful rich
amber color when it
comes out about six
years later—a product
of the oak, the
charring and the warm
Kentucky summers.

Red Whisky.

No one really knows who first made bourbon whisky in Kentucky but we think we might know who made it really drinkable. I think it was the Reverend Elijah Craig—a Baptist minister and former Revolutionary War hero who was also a whisky distiller in the late 1700s.

In 1786, Bourbon County was created from a large piece of what was previously Virginia's Fayette County. Back then, barrels were used to store just about everything including fish, linseed oil and molasses.

Then one day, some think, the frugal Reverend Craig tried to recycle one of these less expensive used barrels by setting fire to the interior to clean it up for reuse. He charred out the inside to eliminate any residue and odor from the former contents.

Then he poured in his whisky and sealed it up.

A magic thing happened. Given a little aging time—say, a long trip down river to New Orleans and a little waiting around—the whisky mellowed out, gained a slight vanilla flavor, a pleasant aroma and a beautiful amber color.

Stamped on the barrel head was its origin—Bourbon County, Kentucky. Folks loved it for its beautiful color and more civilized taste and began to order more of that "Whisky from Bourbon."

We don't know how long it took the Kentucky distillers to get good at this charring and aging thing. But I do know that Gary Regan wrote about an encounter between Abraham Lincoln and Stephen Douglas in 1854 witnessed by James Ewing, who noted the presence of a decanter of "Red Liquor."

Someone had it figured out by then.

(Below) The charring produces a caramel-rich red layer in the wood that adds flavor, aroma and a deep amber color to the whisky over time as it expands and contracts with the changing seasons and moves back and forth through the charred layer and the "red line." The red line is directly behind the char. The apparent red line seen in the center of the wood stave is actually an indication of how far the aging whisky has penetrated into the wood over time.

Balancing the Taste of Maker's Mark.

Every batch of our whisky is a little different, every delivery of white oak barrels is a little different, and every Kentucky season is a little different. That's why you can't bottle whisky based on a computer model. You have to taste it along the way to manage the aging process and you have to taste it to determine when it's ready to go into the bottle.

But, guess what? Every batch is going to be different and if you don't do something about it, your whisky is going to be different bottle-to-bottle when it goes to market. Not a good idea if people expect the taste of Maker's Mark to be the same every time. And they do.

So we have a secret supply of "It." A whisky stash that represents the definitive taste of Maker's Mark. When we have a few batches of mature whisky that we think are ready to bottle, we convene our panel of tasters and sample each one. Our panel is made up of a number of people, but most are women. They seem to have more delicate palates and are able

STANDARD

to determine very subtle differences in the whisky. I would never trust my taste alone.

We compare the taste of every batch against the Maker's Mark standard. Then we combine a sample of this batch and that batch until we find a taste that matches.

Then, and only then, do we combine those specific batches of whisky from the warehouse and begin bottling. It's the only way to ensure that the taste of Maker's Mark will be the same every time you pour it over ice.

Hand-Dipping Each Bottle in Red Sealing Wax.

When my mother talked my father into sealing each bottle of Maker's Mark by hand, one-at-a-time, in hot sealing wax, she forever slowed down the speed of our production line to no more than 38 bottles a minute. This, in an age when production lines of 200, 300, and even 400 bottles per minute were the norm. Not us.

But, there's a good side. The slow line speed affords us the opportunity to carefully inspect each bottle for any imperfections as they go marching by. I think the bottling line goes at just the right speed to ensure that everything is done the way it should be.

Which brings me to the wonderful people who dip each bottle of Maker's Mark. In the old days, they were the wives of our distillery workers. Some still are. But now it seems to be an art form. Really! Each bottle of Maker's Mark is unique. No two are alike. How could they be? Each one is hand-dipped by a unique human being—one at a time.

But they're also like fingerprints. The hot wax translates each person's move-ments and body motion into a virtual signature on the bottle. Although each one is different, sometimes I think I can tell who dipped each bottle.

The Maker's Mark Marketing Plan.

Dad was a hands-on craftsman, not a marketing genius. In fact, I don't think
he knew what marketing was all about. He thought that if you made a good
product, people would search it out and buy it.

So he introduced Maker's Mark in 1958, when bourbon sales were declining
at about 10% a year and the image of bourbon products was maybe at its
lowest point in history. A great time for a new premium product introduction, huh?

We started with one local distributor and Dad's single-minded "Marketing
Strategy"—a belief that if people tried his whisky they would like it and
they, in turn, would tell others about it. You won't find that one at Harvard
Business School, and most marketing directors would say that it's not a real

strategy. Maybe that's why we have never hired a marketing director, even after all these years.

I told Dad a number of times over the years that we needed to be more aggressive marketers but I could never convince him. He thought marketing was rude—sort of like yelling at someone who didn't care much about what you had to say.

We have come to call this whole idea "Discovery." And, that's pretty much how Maker's Mark has grown over the years —friends telling friends about something they found and tasted and liked.

It was slow, but our customers have built our brand, and many whom I've talked to are as proud of Maker's Mark as we are.

Maybe I should call Harvard to see when they want to start the case study.

"Maker's Mark, a boutique bourbon born in a Kentucky hollow, is all the holler among whisky-sippin' connoisseurs."

—James Dodson,
Town & Country

Our First Attempt at Advertising.

it tastes expensive
...and is.

Made from an original old style sour mash recipe by Bill Samuels, fourth generation Kentucky Distiller.

Maker's was a pretty pricey bourbon when it came out in 1958. Most bourbon was stacked up in stores with discount and sale signs attached. Maker's was introduced at $7 a bottle when $3.99 was more the norm.

Mom and Dad were having a little holiday gathering at our home and somebody said, "This whisky sure does taste expensive." Dad responded, "and it is expensive." My mother wrote it down. The next day our first advertising campaign was born. No research. No focus groups. No test marketing—just a jab from a neighbor in our living room.

"My tastes
are very simple.
I only want the
very best of everything."

An eminent British prime minister was quoted as having made that statement.

Sounds great, but for most of us it just isn't possible.

But most of us can enjoy the very best of some things. Among them is whisky.

A lot of people believe that Maker's Mark is the finest whisky to be had.

Though it's not for everyman, it may very well be for you.

Made from an original old style sour mash recipe by Bill Samuels, fourth generation, Kentucky Distiller

Maker's Mark Distillery, Loretto, Ky., Ninety Proof - Fully Matured.

An early magazine ad, about 1970.

Many people still remember our old slogan and ask me about it quite often.

Notice how the view of the bottle never changes even when the art technique changes. Dad finally let us run some ads but he refused to allow us to make a claim of any kind or show his bottle at any angle except exactly like this. He thought this was the most tasteful view.

Our first outdoor board, about 1965.

An early newspaper ad, about 1975.

For the best of friends.
In the best of times.

It tastes expensive...and is.™

Maker's Mark Distillery, Loretto, Ky. Ninety Proof, Fully Matured

What is Sour Mash Whisky? It Doesn't Sound Very Tasty.

Sour mash is an unfortunate term that goes way back in American whisky-making history. It sounds like the whisky would be sour tasting but that's not the case.

It means we use a portion of the grain and water left over from the previous distillation to start the next batch fermenting. It's much the same process that bakers use when making sourdough bread. They hold back some of the finished dough and save it to start the next batch of bread. We call this "backset." We also use it in the cooker for the same reason. It helps to assure a continuity in whisky style, batch to batch, it stabilizes the fermentation, and it provides the

yeast with an ideal medium in which to operate. It also seems to bring additional flavor to the whisky.

We think the process results in a tangible difference in taste and makes for a more consistent product. And it means that each batch of Maker's Mark is related to the one before it and the one before that—all the way back to our first bottle.

We like that, too.

(Below) A fermentation vat.

The Unique Taste of Maker's Mark.

By now, you probably have a feel for all of the things we do at Maker's Mark to craft our whisky differently from other distillers. Dad was after a rich, full flavor and a crisp, clean finish without the lingering aftertaste or bitter overtones normally associated with bourbon whisky. But taste is on the tongue of the beholder and everybody has a personal preference when it comes to taste.

It's also pretty hard to describe a taste sensation. I would say that Maker's Mark is both smooth and complex and has a sweet, succulent mouth feel. I believe it to be the only bourbon that you taste on the end of your tongue where you sense sweetness. The sides of your tongue pick up sour tastes and the back determines bitterness.

We also strive for a balanced taste that is comfortable and pleasant to the palate.

To try it yourself, gather up three or four samples of bourbon brands and cut each to about 60 proof with distilled water. Roll the whisky around on your tongue and breath in through your mouth. How does your tongue feel about it? What do you taste ?

Most people can taste quite a difference between brands and whisky styles.

Well, that's what all the fuss is about and that's why we do things the way we do at Maker's Mark.

Taste.

A Formal Bourbon Tasting.

If you want to conduct a more formal tasting, here are some pointers on how to set it up. Start with a well-lit room. Select three or more whiskies. Don't swallow—spit the whisky out each time to protect your palate. Compare all whiskies on one characteristic before proceeding to the next (i.e., evaluate and compare color before moving to bouquet).

You will need a tasting glass of some sort. A snifter or flute is fine. Even better if you have a separate tasting glass for each different bourbon. And you'll need a glass and a bottle of distilled water for palate cleansing and proof reduction.

Reduce each whisky to 60 proof to allow the flavors to emerge without being overpowered by the alcohol. Rinse your mouth between each taste. Oh, better have someplace to spit.

Use a tasting card like this one as a guide or visit our web site www.makersmark.com and download tasting cards and get more information on organizing your own formal bourbon tasting. Have fun!

SELECTING A FINE BOURBON WHISKY

CHARACTERISTICS		BRAND A	BRAND B	MAKER'S MARK
		SCORE REMARKS	SCORE REMARKS	SCORE REMARKS
	COLOR (7 to 0)			
	BOUQUET (3 to 0)			
	FLAVOR (5 to 0)			
	FINISH (5 to 0)			
	TOTAL			

COLOR
Ideal–Rich and brilliant—flame orange.
Imperfections– Pale or too deep and dark.
Evaluation Procedure– An ounce of whisky is held up to a bright light. Sunlight is preferred.
Score – 2 points (ideal)

BOUQUET
Ideal– Distinctive caramel aroma from the oak and a hint of vanilla. Should smell pleasant and inviting.
Imperfections– Rough, coarse and raw. Smells sour or grain-like. Detectable aroma of burnt wood chips.
Evaluation Procedure– Swirl the whisky in the tasting glass. Allow your nose to go down into the glass and take a rather full inhale.
Score– 3 Points (ideal)

FLAVOR
Ideal– Rich, pleasant flavor. Soft, complex and enjoyable.
Imperfections– Detectable rawness, coarseness, or bite. Or bland and tasteless, like flavored vodka. Or, heavily oak-flavored and rough from over-aging. Sour or grainy tasting from under-aging.
Evaluation Procedure– Take a sip. Roll it around over your tongue for about 5 seconds while breathing in slightly through your mouth. Spit. Wait about 10 seconds, then score.
Score– 5 points (ideal)

FINISH
Ideal– Clean, smooth, and quick. It should leave a satisfying sensation of warmth.
Imperfections– Harsh, burning sensation. A lingering, hard-to-get-rid-of aftertaste. Or, flat without an afterglow.
Evaluation Procedure– Take a sip. Allow the whisky to slide over your tongue and swallow slowly. Relax for 10 to 15 seconds and assess this "last hurrah."
Evaluate and score.
Score– 5 Points (ideal)

The Perfect Mint Julep.

The mint julep may very well be the finest mixed drink in the world.
But hardly anyone has tasted a good one, so it is viewed by most as
a pretty unfortunate taste experience. The problem stems from
three common mistakes people make with mint juleps. The first is
selecting an overbearing bourbon. The second mistake is using too
much mint to cover up the taste of the bourbon. And the last is using
too much sugar in order to make the whole thing drinkable.

This is my mint julep recipe.

Ingredients
1 liter bottle of Maker's Mark
Lots of fresh spearmint
Distilled water
Granulated sugar
Powdered sugar

1. To prepare the mint extract, remove about 40 small mint leaves—wash and place in a small mixing bowl. Cover with 3 ounces of Maker's Mark. Allow the leaves to soak for 15 minutes. Then gather the leaves in a clean, soap-free piece of cotton cloth and vigorously wring the mint bundle over the bowl of whisky. Dip the bundle again and repeat the process several times. Then set aside.

2. To prepare the simple syrup, mix a cup of granulated sugar and a cup of water in a cooking pot. Heat to dissolve the sugar. Stir constantly so the sugar does not burn. Set aside to cool.

3. To prepare the julep mixture, pour 3 1/2 cups of Maker's Mark into a large glass bowl or glass pitcher. (Pour the remaining whisky from the liter bottle into another container and save it for another purpose.) Add 1 cup of the simple syrup to the Maker's Mark.

4. Now, begin adding the mint extract 1 tablespoon at a time to the julep mixture. Each batch of mint extract is different, so you must taste and smell after each tablespoon is added. You may have to leave the room a time or two to clear your nose. The tendency is to use too much mint. You are looking for a soft mint aroma and taste—generally about 3 tablespoons.

5. When you think it's right, pour the whole mixture back into the empty liter bottle and refrigerate it for at least 24 hours to "marry" the flavors.

6. To serve the mint julep, fill each glass (preferably a silver julep cup) half full with shaved ice. Insert a sprig of mint, then pack in more ice to about an inch over the top of the cup. Then, insert a straw that has been cut to one inch above the top of the cup so the nose is forced close to the mint when sipping the julep.

7. When frost forms on the cup, pour the refrigerated julep mixture over the ice and add a sprinkle of powdered sugar to the top of the ice. Then prop your feet up and enjoy.

Our Outdoor Boards.

Over the years, our outdoor advertising has caused quite a stir. Not only is it a major topic of conversation in the communities in which it appears, but I am told that it's been studied by a number of art and advertising classes in high schools and universities. It's also won a remarkable number of professional advertising awards. I wish I could take credit as an advertising genius, but the truth is, we were simply trying to talk with our customers and friends who were already drinking Maker's Mark. So there was no need to say much, or even show the label for that matter. We were just trying to get a nod of approval and maybe a smile. These are some of my favorites.

1988–A formal cocktail party.

1993–Claymation.

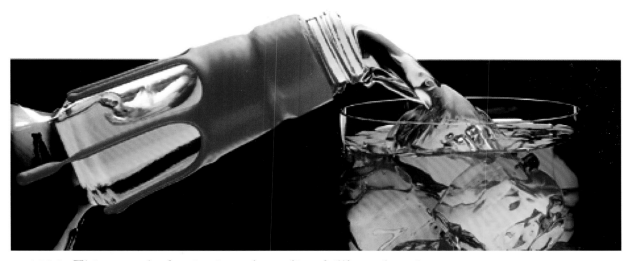

1985–This was the beginning of our first billboard series.

1985

1985

1986–This is the way it evolved.

1986–More.

1986–We just couldn't help ourselves.

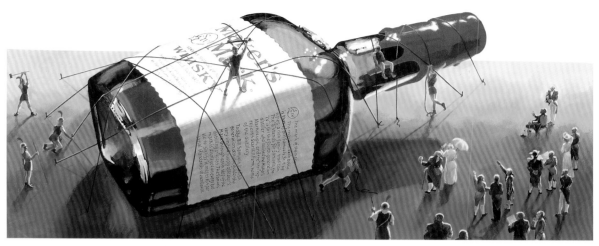

1990—Much discussed and over-analyzed, and called "art."

1990— Even more discussed and over-analyzed.

1990—Never posted and never before published. 3rd in the series.

The great seal of Kentucky.

1997—People wrote to tell us that Maker's was not the great seal of Kentucky, but the great product of Kentucky.

Maker's Mark KENTUCKY STRAIGHT BEER OLD STYLE SOUR MASH — Never happen.

1996—When Jack Daniels came out with a beer of the same name, some of our customers asked if we were next.

1990—The original headline was "Wax eloquent."

Red Neck

Natural Redhead.

1998–Not just another pretty face.

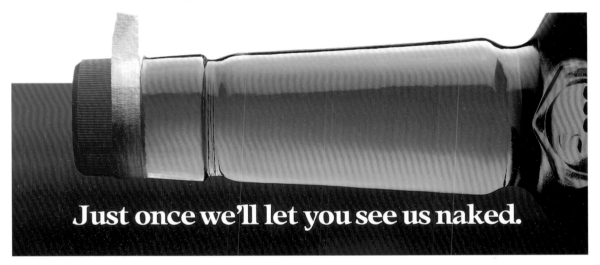

Just once we'll let you see us naked.

1996–Folks seemed to really like this one.

Oooops!

1987–Won the award for best liquor outdoor board in the country.

How Do You Get It Open?

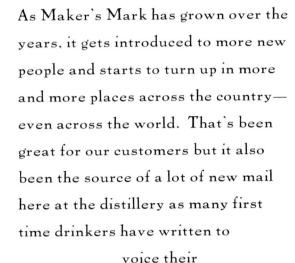

As Maker's Mark has grown over the years, it gets introduced to more new people and starts to turn up in more and more places across the country— even across the world. That's been great for our customers but it also been the source of a lot of new mail here at the distillery as many first time drinkers have written to voice their frustration. Some people are just baffled at how to get the bottle open.

I'm sure we have all run into a bottle in a bar, restaurant, or at someone's home where the wax has been entirely carved off in an effort to get at the whisky.

As the Maker's Mark faithful know, every bottle has a little tab near the top which unseals the cap. Since each bottle is hand dipped, no two are alike, and the tab is sometimes obscured by the sealing wax. But whatever the

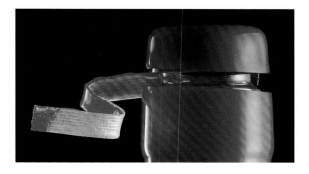

reason, folks sure have come up with some ingenious ways to get it open.

In addition to the carve-it-off approach, people have tried to melt it off, pull it off, and saw it off. One guy even tried to use a chisel.

So, if you see one of those waxless bottles someplace, maybe you could gently suggest the use of the handy pull tab in the future.

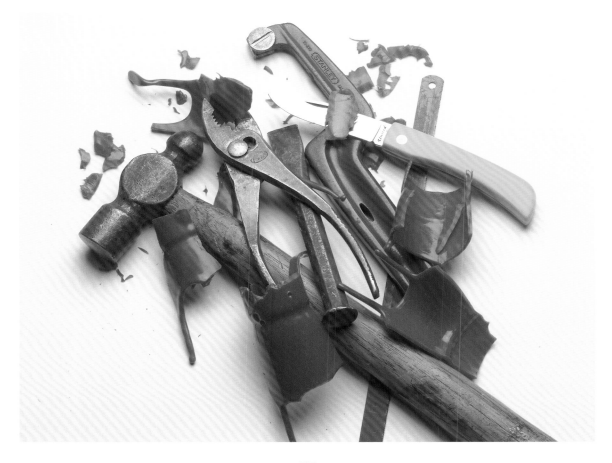

Our New-Found Fame.

One of the most surprising things that has happened over the years since Dad produced that first bottle of Maker's Mark back in the 1950s is the rather remarkable editorial interest that national publications have shown in what we do down here in tiny Loretto, Kentucky.

I think it all started in a big way when The Wall Street Journal published a front page article about us back in August of 1980. People started writing us from all over the country asking where they could buy a bottle of Maker's Mark. Shortly thereafter, other national publications started to nose around to see what all the fuss was about.

Hourly Earnings

HOURLY
Pay - Dollars

7.30 7.10 6.90 6.70 6.50 6.30 5.90 5.70 5.50 5.30

1977 1978 1979 1980

AVERAGE HOURLY PAY of factory workers in June rose to $7.18 from a revised $7.13 the preceding month, the Labor Department reports.

Maker's Mark Goes Against the Grain To Make Its Mark

*   *   *

Bourbon Distiller Is a Model
Of Inefficiency by Choice;
No Case for Fidel Castro

By DAVID P. GARINO
Staff Reporter of THE WALL STREET JOURNAL

LORETTO, Ky.—Maker's Mark Distillery has made its mark by going against the grain.

In producing its premium-priced Maker's Mark bourbon, it continues to use an intricate six-year aging process and a small bottling line that are models of inefficiency. It distills only 19 barrels of bourbon daily, compared with hundreds distilled by other producers. Its ad budget is a meager $1.2 million a year.

But most remarkably, its volume of business has more than tripled, to about 150,000 cases a year, in the past 10 years, while the overall bourbon industry's sales have slipped 26%, to 23.7 million cases.

With its growing reputation for high profitability despite its antiquated production system, Maker's Mark is understandably viewed with envy and lust by some other distillers and conglomerates. But when Maker's Mark is approached by a suitor, says T. William Samuels, chairman, "I just won't talk to them." He represents the fourth generation of his family in the distillery business, and he wants the company to remain

Living and Louisville Lawyer.

Its ad tag line is: "It tastes expensive . . . and is." Typical of its copy: "For those who ask how good a whisky is. Rather than how much."

Origins of the Species

The elder Mr. Samuels got into the distilling business naturally enough. A forebear brewed up whisky for Washington's militia during the Revolutionary War, and the family has seldom been far from that business ever since. Kentucky's leading distillers, the Beams, the Samuelses and John Shaunty, who owned Early Times, lived on the same street, known as "Whisky Row" in Bardstown, about 15 miles from here. Mr. Samuels Jr. recalls sitting on the knee of the leg-

World Bank Approves $67 In Loans to 4

By a WALL STREET Sta

WASHINGTON—The International Development Association, a World Bank approved $67.2 million in loans to tries.

Nepal will get a $27 million cr public water-supply projects in urban while Tanzania will receive a $25 loan for the construction of schools other education facilities.

The IDA also approved two smaller loans—$7.7 million to Burundi and $7.5 million Rwanda—to expand the telephone and telex communications systems in both countries.

All of the IDA credits will be interest-free, except for a small annual administrative fee.

Allis-Chalmers Forms A Venture in Argentina

By a WALL STREET Staff Reporter

MILWAUKEE — Allis-Chalmers Corp. said it formed a venture with Argentina's national shipyard, Astilleros y fabricas Navales S.A., to produce hydraulic turbines and other heavy equipment.

The industrial equipment maker said it hasn't decided how much it will invest in the venture. The venture, called Afne-Allis, plans to build a manufacturing facility about 30 miles south of Buenos Aires.

Allis-Chalmers said last month that it was the apparent low bidder to manufacture 20 hydraulic turbines for a hydroelectric project on $172 million for a hydroelectric project on the Parana River between Argentina and Paraguay. Allis-Chalmers said that if it is awarded that contract, some of the parts would be made at the planned plant.

consle slowly had a ter, dow Now t think it w consumer 9.4% in both delphia's Fide

That's only 1981 bad news: an annual rate o Moreover some say erating before the yea

Surging Food Pric

The price outlook largely because of the prices. The latest evidence the Agriculture Departme day that between mid-Jur farm prices rose 5.2%, one one-month increases on re compounding, that's an annua 62% (see story on page 2).

"Clearly, the drought and i have had a dramatic effect on a prices and commodities inflatic Donald Ratajczak, director of the ec forecasting project at Georgia State sity.

And analysts reason that continued rates of inflation, in turn, will tend to interest rates close to current levels Hunt suggests that the banks' prime the fee charged that their best-rated borrowers "may go back up again." The prime which was reduced to 10% by so last week, may rebound to

Since then we have been featured in the pages of People Magazine, Venture, Business Week, Forbes, Town and Country, Inc. Magazine, The Wine Spectator, Gourmet, Food and Wine, Success Magazine, The New York Times, the Los Angeles Times, Fortune, the Financial Times of London and many, many more.

It's really helped us tell our story and it's helped new people find us.

But what's most gratifying is the fact that editors and writers from all over the country seem to care about what we do and how we do it at Maker's Mark. Our steadfast belief in quality and handmade craftsmanship seem to be values that folks want to share. They come a long way to talk with us and that's almost always the issue they spend the most time on. That makes what we do seem pretty important sometimes.

I like that.

The Manhattan Cocktail.

Story has it that this drink was created in the 1800s at New York City's Manhattan Club. It's a great test of good bourbon and one of my favorite ways to drink Maker's Mark.

1. I like an oversized martini glass like the one shown here, but any type of stemware will do. The important thing is to chill your glass before you start.

2. Fill a mixing glass or cocktail shaker 3/4 full with ice. Add 1 1/2 ounces of Maker's Mark and 1/2 ounce of good quality sweet vermouth. I like to also add a teaspoon of juice from the maraschino cherry jar.

Shake or stir everything up for about 30 seconds.

3. Strain the mixture into your glass and garnish with a maraschino cherry or two. Enjoy.

As Maker's Mark Got Famous, It Started to Rub Off On Me.

I have been president and CEO of Maker's Mark since 1975, and a lot of people associate me with the success of Maker's Mark. But I'll be the first to admit that my great ascent to leadership had very little to do with my ability.

Kentucky Entrepreneur of the Year - 1995 -

 I have done a lot of things to help our cause but dressing in drag as Scarlet O'Hara tops my list.

I was the Boss's son. But my credentials were impeccable. After a less than average academic performance in high school, Dad sent me off to tackle the world of engineering at Case Institute of Technology. There I set a first-semester record. I accumulated the first negative grade point average in the history of this prestigious institution of higher learning.

I did finally graduate and moved on to The University of California at Berkeley. I studied engineering while employed as a design engineer at the Aero Jet General Corporation. Despite some setbacks, I did help design the first-ever non-graphite rocket nozzle used on the Polaris missile. Bingo! I was a "Rocket Scientist." My boss thought not, and suggested I pursue a career in my father's whisky business instead. I mentioned this idea to my father and he sent me to law school to stall my entry into the family business, I'm sure. But I eventually got the chance to learn how to make whisky at my Dad's side.

I get a lot of the credit, but I believe our success comes down to something a little more simple and a little more important than my "marketing genius." Our customers searched out

This is the way I like to think of myself as a seventh-generation distiller. That's my dog, Waxley.

Maker's Mark and shared the discovery with their friends. My father's strategy was to carefully craft a great whisky and then sit back and wait. People eventually found it and liked what they found.

That's how I became famous.

Here I am with my not-so famous race horse, Distiller. (That's me on the left.)

83

Cooking With Maker's Mark.

Professional chefs and country cooks have been telling us for years that Maker's Mark is the best bourbon ever made to cook with. I think it's the lack of "bourbon bite" and the soft, rich, balanced taste that makes it blend so well with food.

Sandra Davis even produced an entire Maker's Mark Cookbook called "That Special Touch." Well, I'm not much of a cook but I do like to eat. Here are four of my favorite Maker's Mark recipes. They taste great and they're easy to make.

Maker's Mark Bourbon Butter

Put it on a steak or put in on a cracker

1 stick of butter
An equal amount of bleu
   cheese
1 Tbs. of Maker's
   Mark (1/2 oz.)

Cream the butter and cheese together at room temperature. Add the bourbon and mix again.

Shape into a ball or press into a small bowl and refrigerate for 24 hours.

Maker's Mark Grilled Steak

(I like T-Bones, but use your favorite steak.)

For each steak—
1 Tbs. olive oil, 1 tsp sage, 1 tsp garlic powder, 1 tsp lemon juice
1 Tbs. Maker's Mark (1/2 oz.)

Place steaks in a deep dish and rub with olive oil.

Crush the sage and rub on both sides. Then sprinkle the bourbon and lemon juice on both sides.

Dust with garlic powder and put the steaks aside to marinate for about 3 hours. Turn them several times.

Cook the steaks over a hot grill to medium or medium rare and try the bourbon butter as a topping on the hot steaks.

Maker's Mark Quart House Baked Beans

2 (1 lb.) cans of your
  favorite baked beans
1 Tbs. Molasses
1/3 cup of strong
  black coffee
1 tsp. dry mustard
1 tsp. brown sugar
1 tsp. onion powder
3 Tbs. Maker's Mark

Put all of the ingredients in a baking dish, stir, cover, and let stand for 3 hours at room temperature.

Preheat oven to 375 degrees. Bake covered for 35 minutes.

Uncover and continue baking for another 30 minutes.

Maker's Mark Bourbon Chocolate Sauce

(Great on ice cream and cake)

2 Tbs. Butter

1 cup granulated sugar

3 Tbs. cocoa

1/4 cup boiling water

2 Tbs. light corn syrup

1/4 tsp. salt

2 Tbs. Maker's Mark

Tweet Yourself.

Melt the butter in a saucepan. Blend the sugar and the cocoa well and add to the melted butter. Add the boiling water slowly and stir constantly. Add the corn syrup and bring the mixture to a boil. Boil for 5 minutes. Then let cool and add the salt and the Maker's Mark.

Note—Keep the leftover sauce refrigerated and heat it up a little before you use it again. It's pretty gooood!

Our History of "Bad" Ads.

It seems like our advertising has been controversial ever since I started helping with it. I'll admit that I am no advertising expert (the folks at our advertising agency will certainly second that motion), but I do know what people want to know about Maker's Mark because I talk to customers every day on the street, on the phone, and at the distillery. I know it's not some trumped-up advertising claim or some cute new ad slogan.

I stay pretty involved because I think what we have to say to our customers is important. But that doesn't mean it has to be serious or full of self-serving puffery. And if we break some advertising rules along the way, OK.

I like an interesting story, so I always wanted our advertising to entertain as well as inform. Mostly what we do is pass along those stories from our friends and customers while trying not to take ourselves too seriously.

We take a lot of criticism about our advertising, and at the same time it wins lots and lots of advertising awards. Go figure. Anyway, here are a few of my favorite ads from the last twenty years. I hope that you can find some of your favorites, and I hope they make you smile at least once.

88

"Your ads need help."
— *M.C., New York, NY*

Boy does that hurt.

The above quote is from a letter I recently received from an executive at one of the world's largest advertising agencies. He apparently saw one of our attempts at self-promotion while flying on Delta Air Lines, where our whisky is served in-flight.

Fortunately, the writer went on to say that the disappointing nature of our ad did not discourage him or his colleagues from ordering and enjoying our whisky while on board. In fact, he says of Maker's Mark, "I'll keep drinking it — despite your ads."

I wish I had someone to blame for our advertising, but that someone would be me. Since our tiny distillery can't afford a big Madison Avenue agency, the task of developing ad ideas falls mainly on my shoulders. And having studied aerospace engineering in college rather than marketing, it seems I just don't have the knack for those snappy slogans.

I guess all this proves conclusively what a friend at an agency in Kentucky once told me: "*Great products sell themselves. It's the ordinary products that need great ads.*"

Bill Samuels, Jr.

Bill Samuels, Jr.
President
Maker's Mark Distillery

Maker's Mark

Maker's Mark Distillery, Loretto, KY 40037, 45% Alc./Vol. (90 Proof), Fully Matured.

After a while, winning so many international "blind" taste competitions gets a little embarrassing. But don't take the word of all those food and wine connoisseurs. Judge for yourself if our whisky's any good. It's available on this Delta Air Lines flight. Just ask for the bourbon with the red wax top.

Bill Samuels, Jr.

Bill Samuels, Jr.
President
Maker's Mark Distillery

Maker's Mark

One of my favorites from 1993.

"My favorite liquor store, Pete's Oasis, has been burglarized on two occasions. Both times, only the Maker's Mark was taken."

–J.B., Apalachicola, FL

I guess we should be flattered that some folks will go to such extremes for a few bottles of our whisky. But robbery may be going a bit far, even for a serious Maker's Mark fan.

After all, we have a tough enough time spreading around what little whisky we make for those willing to acquire it by legal means. And we apologize if you're sometimes unable to find a bottle at your favorite liquor store. Be assured there's always a little more on the way.

Except at Pete's Oasis in Apalachicola, Florida. It seems Pete stopped buying Maker's Mark to keep from being robbed again...and from having his insurance cancelled.

Bill Samuels, Jr.
President
Maker's Mark Distillery

Maker's Mark

Visit us at www.makersmark.com
Maker's Mark Distillery, Loretto, KY 40037, 45% Alc./Vol. (90 Proof), Fully Matured

A great story from 1991.

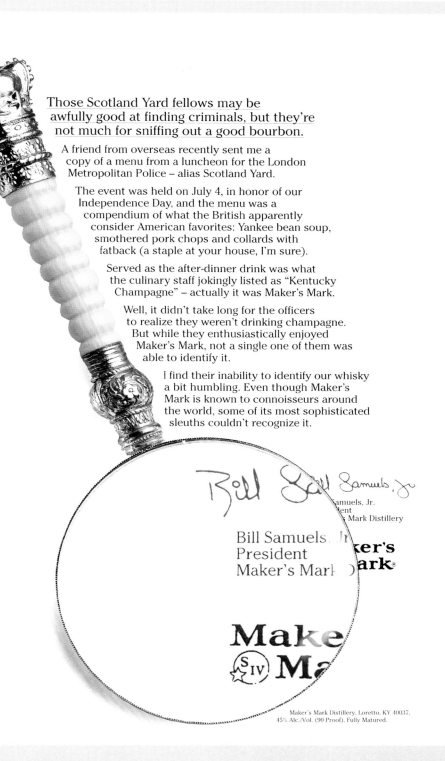

Those Scotland Yard fellows may be awfully good at finding criminals, but they're not much for sniffing out a good bourbon.

A friend from overseas recently sent me a copy of a menu from a luncheon for the London Metropolitan Police – alias Scotland Yard.

The event was held on July 4, in honor of our Independence Day, and the menu was a compendium of what the British apparently consider American favorites: Yankee bean soup, smothered pork chops and collards with fatback (a staple at your house, I'm sure).

Served as the after-dinner drink was what the culinary staff jokingly listed as "Kentucky Champagne" – actually it was Maker's Mark.

Well, it didn't take long for the officers to realize they weren't drinking champagne. But while they enthusiastically enjoyed Maker's Mark, not a single one of them was able to identify it.

I find their inability to identify our whisky a bit humbling. Even though Maker's Mark is known to connoisseurs around the world, some of its most sophisticated sleuths couldn't recognize it.

Bill Samuels, Jr.
President
Maker's Mark Distillery

Bill Samuels, Jr.
President
Maker's Mark

Maker's Mark

Maker's Mark Distillery, Loretto, KY 40037, 45% Alc./Vol. (90 Proof), Fully Matured.

A surprise from 1993.

"Trying to impress a prospective father-in-law who had some considerable doubt as to the quality of this possible son-in-law...

"I bought a bottle of your Maker's Mark.

"After trying your whisky, he had no doubts as to its quality. It was extraordinarily good.

"Unfortunately, he didn't change his opinion about me.

"Worse still, he kept the bottle."

G.B., Canada

A letter writer shared this story with me. I enjoyed it and I thought it well worth sharing with all of you.

Bill Samuels, Jr.
President
Maker's Mark Distillery

Maker's ⓢⱽ Mark®

An early attempt at color in 1985. The Harry Truman look-alike was unintended.

" Stick to making whisky, son.
Your family is distinguished by its
incompetence at doing anything else."
— *J.B., Bardstown, KY*

That was the late Jim Beam's response when
I told him I wanted to pursue a career in
architecture.

He made a good point. My family had been
making whisky in Kentucky for five genera-
tions when along came Prohibition. Like
most distillers of the day, we made a few
attempts at diversification.

All of which turned out to be miserable
failures.

The ventures included forays into newspaper publishing, banking, and a (Franklin)
car dealership — all doomed enterprises
from the start.

I guess it only stands to reason that when we
finally got back into the bourbon business, it
would be with renewed vigor.

When it was my father's turn, he decided to
make a whisky like no other. It would be
delicate and smooth, yet with a distinctive
heartiness all its own.

Fortunately, Dad's instincts about bourbon
were pretty good. Otherwise, I might be
designing houses with roofs of red wax.

Bill Samuels, Jr.

Bill Samuels, Jr.
President
Maker's Mark Distillery

Maker's Mark®

Maker's Mark Distillery, Loretto, KY 40037, 45% Alc./Vol., (90 Proof), Fully Matured

1990—Colonel Jim Beam was my very first mentor.

Merry Ornges.

One weekend a
couple of Christmas
seasons ago, I took my son
Rob (then age 9) to the
office with me while I
worked on our Holiday ad.

There's a spare typewriter
at the office and Rob tried
his hand at it while I was
working. It wasn't until Monday
morning, however, that I
discovered "his" Holiday ad:

"Christmas wishs. i will to
have company cars for
everyone. tell the workers i will
higher paychecks. if it suits give
them time off if knot give
them a basket of ornges.
merry Christmas. Rob."

Naturally when I got
home that Monday evening,
I mentioned that I had found his
ad. And I asked him what he thought
we should do about it.

"Put it in the paper," he suggested hopefully.

Merry ornges to all and to all a good night.

Bill Samuels, Jr.
Bill Samuels, Jr.
President
Maker's Mark Distillery

Maker's Mark

Malcolm Forbes called this the best business ad of 1982.

The London Times said of Maker's Mark, "What separates this bourbon from the rest is the softness and smoothness of its rich oak, vanilla and raisiny-like caramel flavours."

I don't know what that means, but it sounds great.

This tribute from Jane MacQuitty, spirits writer for the *London Times*, has my head spinning a bit. I think what she's saying is that she likes our whisky, but I'm not quite sure.

I wasn't there at the time my Dad created the whisky that became Maker's Mark, but I can't ever remember him talking about raisins or vanilla or caramel. Except maybe when he took my sister and me to the neighborhood ice cream parlor.

The part about the softness and smoothness of Maker's Mark sounds a bit more familiar. Dad chose winter wheat for his whisky instead of the traditional rye to give it those very qualities.

I'm glad that Ms. MacQuitty found it to her liking, because judging from her comments about Maker's Mark, her palate is every bit as sophisticated as her prose. And praise for our whisky from those who really appreciate fine bourbons is always welcome.

Even when it goes way over my head.

Bill Samuels, Jr.

Bill Samuels, Jr.
President
Maker's Mark Distillery

Maker's Mark®

Maker's Mark Distillery, Loretto, KY 40037, 45% Alc./Vol. (90 Proof), Fully Matured

Some pretty rich and creamy language from 1992. But a great way to think about taste.

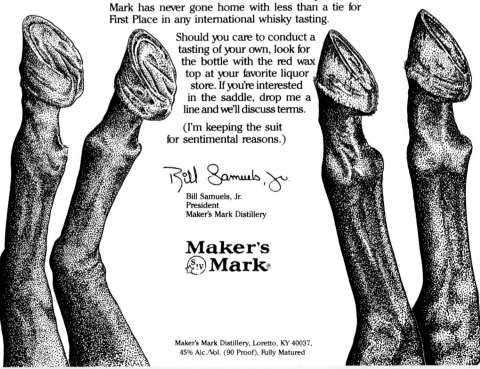

For sale: one (barely) used saddle.

Here in Kentucky, probably the only field more people claim expertise in than bourbon whisky is horse racing. So when a couple of friends came to me offering partial ownership of what they described as a "can't-miss," born-for-the winner's circle thoroughbred, I just couldn't resist.

I paid my money, ordered some lovely racing silks, and bought a white suit to look good for the TV cameras come Derby Day.

Alas, not for us the blanket of roses. After finishing last, last and seventh in its first three races, the horse died. Leaving these three would-be syndicators with about 300 lbs. of uneaten oats and a nearly-new, custom saddle.

I did learn a valuable lesson, though: spend your time and money on things you know. Which in my case is crafting whisky and definitely not racing horses. For while our horse finished out of the money, Maker's Mark has never gone home with less than a tie for First Place in any international whisky tasting.

Should you care to conduct a tasting of your own, look for the bottle with the red wax top at your favorite liquor store. If you're interested in the saddle, drop me a line and we'll discuss terms.

(I'm keeping the suit for sentimental reasons.)

Bill Samuels, Jr.

Bill Samuels, Jr.
President
Maker's Mark Distillery

Maker's Mark®

Maker's Mark Distillery, Loretto, KY 40037,
45% Alc./Vol. (90 Proof), Fully Matured

This ad got me into a whole lot of deserved trouble with the Kentucky thoroughbred folks in 1988.

It's amazing what some people will go through for a drink of good whisky.

A few weeks ago, we received a letter that truly attests to the loyalty of some of our customers. And, like myself, if you ever had your mouth washed out with soap, you can almost taste the experience I'm about to describe.

It seems that Jim and some friends were preparing for a week of fly-fishing in Montana. Jim wasn't about to leave his Maker's Mark behind, but he couldn't risk a broken bottle in his duffle bag. Thinking like a true outdoorsman, Jim rinsed out an old plastic shampoo bottle and filled it with his beloved whisky.

Unfortunately for Jim, shampoo has a habit of working its way into plastic. Still, rather than settle for the lesser brand one of his friends had brought along, Jim stuck with his soapy Maker's Mark through the duration of the week.

To some, it may sound like Jim's a few bricks shy of a load, but personally, we're flattered. I like to think it proves our customers simply prefer soapy Maker's Mark to none at all.

Bill Samuels, Jr.

Bill Samuels, Jr.
President
Maker's Mark Distillery

Maker's Ⓢ IV Mark®

A great testimonial from 1992.

What kind of spirits are conjured up at Kentucky's "House of Wax"?

I've always thought it odd that over in London, England, people line up every day to see lifelike wax sculptures of famous people at a place called Madame Tussaud's. I find the whole idea of people made out of wax a bit creepy. Maybe it's because I saw that Vincent Price movie "House of Wax" as a kid. I don't know.

But I do know there must be something interesting about wax because so many visitors to our little distillery want to see where we hand-dip our bottles of Maker's Mark. They seem to be fascinated by the way wax drips down each bottle, personalizing each and every one of them with a unique design.

Of course, we've got lots of other things to see at our completely restored distillery. It's the only one in America declared a National Historic Landmark.

So, if you'd like to visit, just call Donna at 502-865-2099 for directions. And if you get lost in the rolling hills around Loretto, Kentucky, just ask anyone you meet to direct you to the House of Wax.

They'll know exactly what you're talking about.

Bill Samuels, Jr.
Bill Samuels, Jr.
President
Maker's Mark Distillery

Maker's Mark

Maker's Mark Distillery, Loretto, KY 40037, 45% Alc./Vol. (90 Proof), Fully Matured

That's me in the window c. 1985.

I love this 1995 ad because I love the old letterpress.

Maker's Mark is the only bourbon
to use water exclusively from
natural limestone springs.

Our gardener
remains
unimpressed.

The spring-fed
lake out behind our
little distillery has been
serving double-duty for some
years now. Not only is it a big
part of our bourbon's unique
taste, it supplies our gardener
(who also happens to be my
brother-in-law, Russ) with a
steady supply of natural spring
water for his roses.

Now, I take as much pride as
anybody in maintaining the
beauty of the distillery's
landscaping, but we've had a heck
of a time trying to cope with an
ever-growing demand for our whisky.
With only so much spring water to go
around, I decided something had to give.
For the time being, and much to the dis-
may of Russ and his American Beauties,
it was the landscaping.

Fortunately, soon after this decision was
made, the local authorities consented to run
a water line out to us for our everyday
needs. Now the natural spring water is being
used exclusively on what I'm convinced it
was meant for – Maker's Mark. And though
he's having to get by with plain tap water,
Russ seems happier, too.

Bill Samuels, Jr.

Bill Samuels, Jr.
President
Maker's Mark Distillery

Maker's
Mark

This ad smoothed things over with my brother-in-law in 1993.

<u>In certain circles, the man on the right is viewed as the real revolutionary.</u>

I know because he's my father, as well as the father of Maker's Mark.

In 1953, our family had been in the whisky business for nearly two centuries. Frankly, the old family brand was not much different from the hundreds of other whisky brands. It was somewhat harsh and a little rough around the edges.

Dad wanted no part of that. So he did something that not only turned things upside down within the family, but throughout the entire whisky industry as well. He threw out the 170-year-old family recipe and started over.

And, if that weren't radical enough, Dad intended to replace it with something considered impossible in those days – a smooth, agreeable, premium bourbon. To bring about his "crackpot idea," Dad substituted gentler winter wheat for the usual rye. And used only water from a limestone, spring-fed lake on the grounds of the tiny old distillery he'd bought for his experiment.

After letting his bourbon age for about 6 years, he found that his instincts were correct. Admittedly, what he did wasn't as earthshaking as the Chinese or Russian revolutions. But here in bourbon country, it was downright cataclysmic.

Bill Samuels, Jr.

Bill Samuels, Jr.
President
Maker's Mark Distillery

Maker's
(S IV) Mark®

We received a lot of bad mail on those other two guys we put in with dad in this 1992 ad. But dad loved this ad. I sure was glad.

"Bartender! Another shot of redeye for my friend."

You may have heard people say they dislike bourbon. I think I've figured out why.

When this nation was wild and woolly, men coming off the trail were not in the mood for a mild-mannered whisky.

Back then, if it didn't "blow your ears off," it just wasn't considered fit to drink.

Well, my father wasn't interested in making bourbon the way it was supposed to taste. He wanted to create a good-natured, mild-mannered whisky.

Maybe that's why, even today, a lot of folks tell us they don't like bourbon, but they sure do enjoy the taste of Maker's Mark.

Bill Samuels, Jr.
President
Maker's Mark Distillery

Maker's (SIV) Mark

Maker's Mark Distillery, Loretto, KY 40037, 45% Alc./Vol. (90 Proof), Fully Matured

A really fun ad from 1989.

"Remember me??

I've written you two letters in the past. One about finding Maker's Mark for the first time in Oregon and the second about finding your whisky in California. (I must have searched all over. And it's an even bigger state than Oregon.)

"Well, I've moved again. In fact, I've traveled and settled half way around the world. My new home is Perth, Australia. And right now you're probably thinking I'm going to ask you where to find Maker's Mark down here. (And Australia is even bigger than California.) But, I'm not.

"Because the other day I was reading an article on whiskies in *Follow me Gentlemen* (it's Australia's version of *GQ*) and it said: 'The best bourbon is Maker's Mark, if you can find it.'

"How about that. I just get here and practically the first thing I read tells me I can't find it. Little do they realize how much practice I already have."

—*T.K., Australia*

Maker's
⟨S IV⟩ Mark

Our ads go international in 1985.

Some who visit our distillery could care less about the taste of Maker's Mark.

Some just drop in for a visit on their way to somewhere else. The ducks from up North, for instance, seem to like our natural spring-fed lake – the only source of water we use in Maker's Mark. But that's about the extent of their interest in our whisky.

On the other hand, all the people who stop by our little "National Historic Landmark" find the trip worthwhile. From the old Quart House and Toll Gate House, to the "still" house, with its hand-polished copper still, hand-hewn support beams and 100-plus-year-old hardwood floor, there's nothing about the place that doesn't show the same personal care that goes into Maker's Mark.

Even the beautiful, pre-Civil War distiller's residence is a curiosity. It now serves as our Visitor's Center, with its mingled collections of Kentucky arts, crafts, and period furniture from the early 1800's.

And besides, we enjoy having folks (and ducks) around the distillery – every bit as much as we like making our award-winning whisky.

So, even if you're not the least bit interested in whisky, we'd still love to have you drop in for a visit. Just call Donna at (502) 865-2099 or stop by Monday–Saturday, 10:30 a.m.-3:30 p.m.

Maker's Mark Distillery
Loretto, KY 40037
45% Alc./Vol.
(90 Proof)
Fully Matured

Bill Samuels, Jr.

Bill Samuels, Jr.
President
Maker's Mark Distillery

Maker's (S IV) Mark®

Some of our friends don't drink—1991.

104

Whoops.

Maker's Mark is handmade every step of the way,
as exemplified by the red wax that delicately
trickles down the neck of each bottle.

Well, most of them anyway.

President

Maker's
(S IV) Mark®

Maker's Mark Distillery, Loretto, KY 40037, 45% Alc./Vol. (90 Proof), Fully Matured

This 1995 ad created an overnight demand for over-dipped bottles of
Maker's Mark. You will find them occasionally on display in bars and
restaurants across the country.

At first, I didn't believe it myself.

Not too long ago, I received a phone call from a woman in Hattiesburg, Mississippi, whose real name is Mrs. Jack Daniel.

She told me that for years, and for obvious reasons, the only whisky her husband, Jack Daniel, would drink was the one with his name. Convinced her husband was too stubborn for his own good, Mrs. Daniel spent quite some time trying to get her husband to at least consider other brands. Finally, after years of friendly prodding, Jack consented to give our whisky a try. Now, according to Mrs. Daniel, Maker's Mark is the only whisky Jack Daniel drinks.

Well, I was so tickled by her story that for a brief instant I considered leaking it to one of those supermarket tabloids. Fortunately for Mr. and Mrs. Daniel, I came to my senses.

Of course, I'm not surprised that Jack Daniel prefers Maker's Mark. We've won over many converts to our smooth, handcrafted bourbon, once they tried it.

But, to like it enough to give up the chance to order a fine whiskey that bears your own name... well, I guess that says more about our bourbon than I ever could.

Bill Samuels, Jr.
President
Maker's Mark Distillery

Maker's
(S IV) Mark®

Scam 95¢/99¢ CANADA Vol. 1 - No. 1 - 1993

Space Aliens Ate My Baby!

JACK DANIEL DRINKS MAKER'S MARK

MELON HEADED MAN SPEAKS ALIEN TONGUE
Uses hand signals to communicate with police and army officials

JESSE JAMES FOUND ALIVE IN LORETTO, KENTUCKY

Woman Marries Wildebeast!

1993–My friends who make Jack Daniels did not think this was very funny.

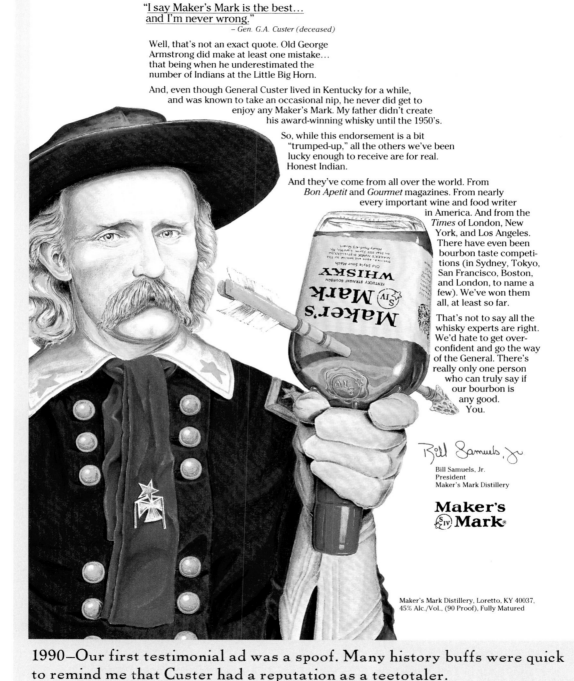

"I say Maker's Mark is the best...
and I'm never wrong."
– *Gen. G.A. Custer (deceased)*

Well, that's not an exact quote. Old George Armstrong did make at least one mistake... that being when he underestimated the number of Indians at the Little Big Horn.

And, even though General Custer lived in Kentucky for a while, and was known to take an occasional nip, he never did get to enjoy any Maker's Mark. My father didn't create his award-winning whisky until the 1950's.

So, while this endorsement is a bit "trumped-up," all the others we've been lucky enough to receive are for real. Honest Indian.

And they've come from all over the world. From *Bon Apetit* and *Gourmet* magazines. From nearly every important wine and food writer in America. And from the *Times* of London, New York, and Los Angeles. There have even been bourbon taste competitions (in Sydney, Tokyo, San Francisco, Boston, and London, to name a few). We've won them all, at least so far.

That's not to say all the whisky experts are right. We'd hate to get over-confident and go the way of the General. There's really only one person who can truly say if our bourbon is any good. You.

Bill Samuels, Jr.

Bill Samuels, Jr.
President
Maker's Mark Distillery

Maker's Mark (S IV S) ®

Maker's Mark Distillery, Loretto, KY 40037,
45% Alc./Vol., (90 Proof), Fully Matured

1990—Our first testimonial ad was a spoof. Many history buffs were quick to remind me that Custer had a reputation as a teetotaler.

Our Collector Bottles Raise Big Money for Charity.

Back in 1993, we dipped a few bottles of Maker's Mark in blue wax and it caused quite a stir.

So in 1996, we made a white wax bottle to cheer on the Kentucky Wildcats and raise some money for charity and it worked. The Wildcats won the NCAA basketball championship and the bottle became a trophy that each fan could own. We made over 100,000 of them.

We were able to contribute $255,000 to the Daniel Pitino Foundation for disadvantaged children of Kentucky.

In 1998, we went to work for the University of Louisville on the occasion of its 200th anniversary and produced a special black wax U of L bottle and donated the profits to the School of Education for scholarships. Both my mother and father were U of L graduates and it was a great opportunity for me to give something back to the University.

That felt so good we tried it again. We started a sponsorship program in 1997 with Keeneland Race Track in Lexington, Kentucky. We sponsored a Grade II stakes race called The Maker's Mark Mile and Keeneland asked if we could do a special limited bottling for them. All profits would go to the Keeneland Foundation.

We did a Keeneland bottle in 1997, 1998 and 1999. They always sold out in just a few days. But when they came to us for a 2000 edition, we had to decline. The demand for Maker's Mark had put our limited capacity to the test and we did not feel we could spare the whisky for another collector bottle. "So what," they said, "Just give us a bottle. Nobody opens them anyway. They're too collectable."

So we did. And, by golly, those wonderful customers and race fans lined up and bought them anyway—all 10,000 empty bottles. We donated all the proceeds to charity and came away quite humbled by the whole experience.

Over the years it's been fun. But I think we're done. We have barely enough whisky to fill our regular red wax bottles now, so unfortunately we have no plans for any more collector bottles. After the 2001 Keeneland bottle.

| 1997 | 1998 | 1999 | 2000 |

Some things that we have done over the years have drawn a lot of comment from our friends and customers.

This is the introduction of our Small Batch Bourbon Collection—poking a little fun at the new Gucci®-inspired, high-priced designer bourbons.

We made some blue wax seals for the Commonwealth of Kentucky and had some wax left over. So, just for fun, we dipped some bottles. Well, people went crazy. Some who bought them resold them for over $200.

Today I am told that they sell for as much as $2,000 at auction. We promised never to make another blue wax liter bottle—ever.

A customer in the military sent us this hand painted bottle but told us it would be hard to find on the shelf.

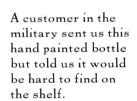

Celebrating my favorite comedian's birth. From an outdoor board in 1990.

110

(Right) A friend built this handmade glass Christmas ornament filled with Maker's Mark after being inspired by our holiday outdoor board (above).

How about this for a bottle cover to keep your Maker's Mark warm on a long cold winter's night?

This is what our garden party will be like. Except it's not on Sunday, not in France and our butts don't stick out.

This was a poster-size invitation to a brunch at the distillery during Kentucky Derby week 1998.

A nip in the bud.

(Left) Our customers loved this one and covered us up with requests for copies.

(Right) A dazzling spring bouquet of fine, slowly-aged Kentucky bourbon.

1997. A poster in honor of new University of Kentucky football coach Hal Mumme.

Mark Of A Great Coach.

A poster in honor of new University of Kentucky basketball coach "Tubby" Smith, 1997.

Mark of a great coach.

Some folks will go to great lengths to make sure they have a supply of Maker's Mark when they travel.

Jack Daniels stops by our house for a drink in 1994 and tells us he prefers Maker's Mark.

This is the much-discussed Maker's Mark corset bottle. It was designed for an invitation and I thought it was really fun and entertaining. But our advertising and public relations agency was shocked and pleaded for better judgment. We didn't use it, but I could not resist using it here. I still think it's clever and amusing.

This is the formal escort for our corset bottle. Don't we clean up nice?

Please come and see us.

We're pretty much off the beaten path so we're really delighted when people take the time and trouble to come to visit us. We would love to show you around our little National Historic Landmark distillery and give you a personal look at how we handcraft Maker's Mark from start to finish. We're proud of our home and we are proud of what we do here. We would be very pleased to share it with you.

Also, you'll find a lot of nifty merchandise in our gift gallery. We have everything from jackets to julep cups, including t-shirts, glassware, golf stuff and cookbooks. You can even get a small bottle of Maker's Mark and try your hand at dipping it in red sealing wax the same way that we do. It's harder than it looks but it makes a great keepsake of your visit.

114

If you can't come by to see us in person, visit us at www.makersmark.com. It's full of information about Maker's Mark as well as other bourbons. We try to keep it updated with anything new that's going on and it's a great place to ask a question or let me know what you think about the book, the bourbon, or anything else you have on your mind.

Tour Information

Free tours are conducted at 10:30 a.m., 11:30 a.m., 12:30 p.m., 1:30 p.m., 2:30 p.m., and 3:30 p.m. Monday through Saturday year-round. Sunday tours are conducted at 1:30 p.m., 2:30 p.m., and 3:30 p.m. Open holidays except Easter Sunday, Thanksgiving, Christmas Eve, Christmas Day, and New Year's Day. Our gift gallery is open the same hours and days.

For more information, contact our Visitor Center, Marker's Mark Distillery, Loretto, Kentucky 40037 270-865-2099.

You can write to me, Bill Samuels, at the same address.

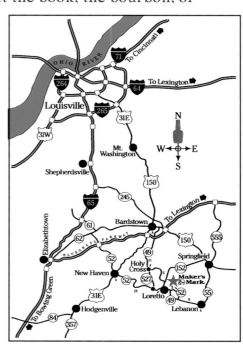

CREDITS

- Covers–Warren Lynch Photography, Louisville, KY.
- Title Page–Warren Lynch Photography.
- Dedication–Warren Lynch Photography
- Introduction–Seal by Warren Lynch Photography. Photo by Dan Dry Photography, Louisville, KY
- Pages 10-11–Derrick Grinnel Illustration.
- Pages 12-13–Warren Lynch Photography.
- Pages 14-15–Warren Lynch Photography.
- Pages 16-17–Warren Lynch Photography.
- Pages 18-19–Seal photo by Warren Lynch; B&W photo by Lin Caufield, Louisville, KY. Bottle photo by Mathew Brady.
- Pages 20-21–Illustration by Chuck Slack. Photography by Warren Lynch.
- Pages 22-23–Painting by David McCall Johnson, Franklin, MI.
- Pages 24-25–Bridge photo by John Beckman, Clarksville, IN. All others by Dan Dry Photography.
- Pages 26-27–Dan Dry photos.
- Page 28–Charlie Westerman Photography, Chicago, IL.
- Page 29–B&W by Lin Caufield. Color by Jim Lindsey, Louisville, KY.
- Pages 30-31–Vintage photos from the Maker's Mark Collection. Handgun from the John Walker Collection. Photography by Warren Lynch.
- Pages 32-33–Jessie and Frank photos and handgun are from the Maker's Mark Collection. The Kearney photo is from the John Walker Collection. All copy photos are by Warren Lynch.
- Pages 34-35–Illustration by Cynthia Torp, Louisville, KY. Photographs by Warren Lynch.
- Pages 36-37–Barrels and bottle photography by Warren Lynch. Warehouse and tasting photos by Dan Dry.
- Pages 38-39–Illustration by Chuck Slack. Photography by Warren Lynch.
- Pages 40-41–Photos by Warren Lynch.
- Pages 42-43–Claymation photography by Jack Graham, Phoenix, AZ. Hand photography by Dan Dry.
- Pages 44-45–Dan Dry Photography.
- Pages 46-47–Dan Dry Photography.
- Pages 48-49–Dan Dry Photography.
- Pages 50-51–Illustration by Chuck Slack. Warehouse photo by Dan Dry. Bung and glasses photography by Warren Lynch.
- Pages 52-53–Warren Lynch Photography.
- Pages 54-55–Bottle and glass photography by Warren Lynch. Tasting photo by Dan Dry.
- Pages 56-57–Warren Lynch Photography.
- Pages 58-59–Warren Lynch Photography.
- Pages 60-61–Ads by Doe-Anderson Advertising, Inc, Louisville, KY. Photography by Mathew Brady. Illustration by Don Reibert, Louisville, KY.
- Pages 62-63–Bottle photo by Mathew Brady. Factory photos by Dan Dry.
- Pages 64-65–Warren Lynch Photography.
- Page 66–Warren Lynch Photography.
- Page 68–Warren Lynch Photography.
- Page 70–Bears by Cynthia

Torp Illustration. Cat by Jack Graham Claymation and Photography.
- Page 71–All photographs by Warren Lynch Photography.
- Page 72–"And" by Warren Lynch Photography. "On" and "Over" by Cynthia Torp Illustrations.
- Page 73–All by Mark Cable Illustrations, Louisville, KY.
- Page 74–All photographs by Warren Lynch Photography.
- Page 75–"Redhead" and "Naked" by Warren Lynch Photography. "Oooops" by Cynthia Torp Illustration.
- Pages 76-77–Warren Lynch Photography.
- Pages 78-79–Warren Lynch Photography.
- Page 80–Warren Lynch Photography.
- Page 82–Warren Lynch Photography.
- Page 83–Horse photo by Warren Lynch Photography. White Suit photo by Julian Calder, The United Kingdom.
- Page 84–Jim Gastinger Illustration, Louisville, KY.
- Page 85–Warren Lynch

Photography.
- Pages 86-87–Photos by Warren Lynch. Claymation photo by Jack Graham.
- Page 89–Ad by Doe-Anderson Advertising, Inc., Louisville, Kentucky. Photography by Warren Lynch.
- Pages 90-91–Ads by Doe-Anderson Advertising. Illustration by Chuck Slack. Photography by Warren Lynch.
- Pages 92-93–Ads by Doe-Anderson Advertising. Illustration by Pip Pullen, Louisville, KY. Photography by Warren Lynch.
- Pages 94-95–Ads by Doe-Anderson Advertising. Photography by Warren Lynch.
- Pages 96-97–Ads by Doe-Anderson Advertising. Illustration by Don Reibert, Louisville, KY. Photography by Warren Lynch.
- Pages 98-99–Ads by Doe-Anderson Advertising. Illustration by Cynthia Torp. Photography by Warren Lynch.
- Pages 100-101–Ads by Doe-Anderson Advertising. Illustration by Don Riebert. Photography by Warren Lynch.
- Pages 102-103–Ads by Doe-Anderson Advertising. Illustration by Chuck Slack. Photography by Warren Lynch.
- Pages 104-105–Ads by Doe-Anderson Advertising. Illustration by Chuck Slack. Photography by Warren Lynch.
- Pages 106-107–Ads by Doe-Anderson Advertising. Illustration by Don Reibert. Photography by Warren Lynch.
- Pages 108-109–Warren Lynch Photography.
- Page 110–Illustrations by Don Reibert. Photography by Warren Lynch.
- Page 111–Photography by Warren Lynch.
- Page 112–Photography by Warren Lynch.
- Page 113–Photography by Warren Lynch.
- Pages 114-115–Sign photo by Jim Lindsey; Distillery photo by Dan Dry; Map Illustration by Don Reibert.
- Page 116–Warren Lynch Photography.
- For more information on Sandra Davis's Maker's Mark Cookbook call (859) 336-7749.